Library and Archives Canada Cataloguing in Publication

Perreault, Joyce, 1967-, author
All creation represented : a child's guide to the medicine
wheel / Joyce Perreault.

ISBN 978-0-9950127-1-4 (softcover)

1. Medicine wheels--Juvenile literature.  I. Title.

BF1623.M43P47 2017          j299.7          C2017-904723-X

Peppermint Toast Publishing
New Westminster, BC, Canada
www.pepperminttoast.com

Edited by Grayson Smith and Cailey Morgan
Design by Kristin Church

ISBN: 978-0-995012714

*All Creation Represented: A Child's Guide to the Medicine Wheel* was printed in China using SoySeal quality inks on Forest Stewardship Council® certified paper by fairly compensated, adult employees who are protected by the Workplace Conditions Assessment.

# ALL CREATION REPRESENTED

*A Child's Guide to the Medicine Wheel*

I want to acknowledge my mother and father for
teaching us how to live off the land and for teaching
us to love everyone as they are.

I would like to acknowledge all Elders that have taught
and continue to teach the ways of our people.

I wish to acknowledge the Elder who gave us his knowledge,
as a gift of wisdom for the children who read it, and to respect
his wish for privacy — Miigwetch.

Additional special thanks to those who have
provided valuable insight and input:

**Robert Clifton**, Liimk Halaayt - Gitga'at Tsimshian
**Catee Rose**, Three Fires Confederacy of Minido Minis (Spirit Island
aka Manitoulin Island)
**Debora Abood**, author, *Precious and Sacred* Series

To all Indigenous People that are searching
for their ancestral roots.

And to my patient and loving family:
my husband Daniel, my children,
and my grandbabies.

May our Creator bless everyone.
Joyce Perreault

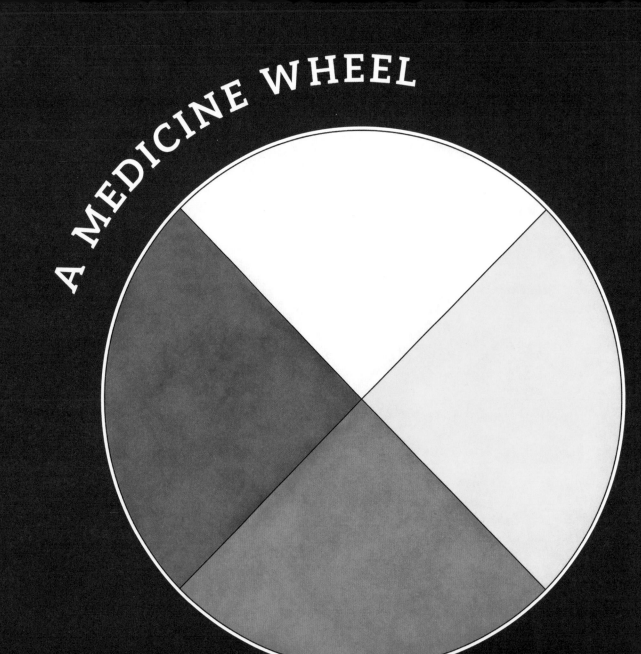

A MEDICINE WHEEL

# WHAT IS A MEDICINE WHEEL?

A Medicine Wheel is a foundation of teaching and learning that shows how different parts of life are connected and balanced. The symbol of four colours in a circle represents the interconnectivity of all aspects of a person's relationship with themselves, others, and the natural and spiritual worlds.

Some cultures may view the order and significance of the concepts differently from one another, but what stays the same is that all creation is represented on the Wheel. The Anishinaabe, or Ojibwe People, have a teaching that the Medicine Wheel is the Circle of Life. From generation to generation, the Medicine Wheel gives us a place in the universe and clarifies our relationship to Mother Earth.

This book teaches about the Medicine Wheel from an Ojibwe perspective.

THE SACRED NUMBER FOUR

# FOUR IS A SACRED NUMBER.

The Medicine Wheel is made up of four parts. Many things in the natural world are represented in four ways, such as the Directions, the Elements, the Seasons, and the Times of Day. Some cultures have sacred knowledge about the Animals and the Plants. A person is often represented in four ways as well, such as in the Nations, the Aspects of a Human Being, and the Stages of Life.

Four is a sacred number for the Ojibwe People. We have many cultural practices that include the sacred number four, such as the number of rounds of drumming, rounds of singing, or rounds of being in a sweat lodge.

# THE FOUR DIRECTIONS

where we rest and remember

**NORTH**

where we come from

**EAST**

where we ripen and prepare for harvest

**WEST**

where we grow, search, and dance

**SOUTH**

# WHEN WE LOOK AT A WORLD MAP, WE SEE THE FOUR DIRECTIONS CLEARLY.

Our ancestors knew and believed that the Directions unified the whole world.

The East is where we come from. In the East, we learn kindness, open-mindedness, innocence, and leadership.

The South is where we grow, search, and dance. In the South, we learn to work, help our families, and live off the land.

The West is where we ripen with age and prepare for harvest. In the West, we learn to see everyone as equal through the Creator.

The North is the place of wisdom where we rest and remember. In the North, we learn strength, truth, and wisdom.

air

earth

water

fire

THE FOUR ELEMENTS

# ALL THE ELEMENTS ARE NECESSARY, AND WE HONOUR THEM WITH GRATITUDE FOR SUPPORTING LIFE.

Water is in the East. Rivers, oceans, and watersheds are considered the veins of Mother Earth. All living things require clean Water to survive. As people, we are formed in the amniotic fluid we call Water and are born out of it. When we cry, our tears cleanse us. Before we finish our day, we cleanse ourselves with Water.

Fire is in the South. Energy from the sun is the basis of all food chains. Fire, including the electricity we use today, keeps us warm, lights our homes, and allows us to cook food. Our ancestors used Fire and the sun to cook food, dry meats, and make pemmican when there was no electricity for cooking or light.

Earth is in the West. Plants require soil and minerals to grow, and the soil requires plants and animals to stay healthy. Mountains, plains, and even deserts support this interconnected life. We all love to eat fruits and vegetables, and Earth allows us to eat them fresh daily. We love to look at trees and flowers — Earth allows us to admire them, too.

Air is in the North. All life on Earth needs Air to breathe. It is essential to life. We must preserve our clean Air, as all living things depend on it. Air is the first breath we take when we are born and the last breath we take when we move on to the spirit world.

# THE FOUR SEASONS

winter

autumn

spring

summer

# THE SEASONS TEACH US HOW TIME AND THE PHYSICAL WORLD BRING INNER REGENERATION.

Spring is in the East. Spring brings new beginnings, the dawn of a new day, and birth. Innocence, vulnerability, and curiosity can be found or reclaimed during this season. New growth, fresh plants, and new baby animals are seen during Spring.

Summer is in the South. Just like the rapid growth that occurs during this season, Summer is full of great beauty and intensity. The heat can leave us feeling out of breath and thirsty. The lessons we learn in Summer happen quickly, and by the time it's over, it feels like it just began.

Autumn is in the West. Autumn is when we reap the harvest of the food we planted. The trees change their colour and lose their leaves. Animals burrow down for the cold, long nights to come. We hope that the harvest will sustain us through the long sleep of Winter until Spring arrives. Autumn is a return to the womb of creation.

Winter is in the North. Winter is a time to give back and share our wisdom with others. The North is a beautiful place of rest and healing. Many people want to leave the fast-paced city for the strong silence of the North — a place that heals us from everyday life and its frustrations.

night

evening

sunrise

noon

THE FOUR TIMES OF DAY

# THE TIMES OF DAY TEACH US HOW TO INTERACT IN HARMONY WITH OUR NATURAL SURROUNDINGS.

Sunrise is in the East. The Ojibwe People built their tiipiis with the door facing the East, to be warmed by the morning sun.

Noon is in the South. The highpoint of the sun told our ancestors that while work was not yet over, it was time to prepare the feast for celebration.

Evening is in the West. In the days of our ancestors, there were no clocks to tell them when the workday was over. They toiled until the sun set in the West.

Night is in the North. Another day has come and gone, and rest from hard work is finally here. Night gives time for peace and admiration of the Northern Lights, the stars, and the moon, which belong in the North.

THE FOUR SACRED ANIMALS

white bear

buffalo

eagle

deer

# EACH SACRED ANIMAL CONNECTS US TO OUR CULTURE.

Eagle is in the East. The Eagle flies the highest, sees the farthest, and is closest to the Creator. Eagle feathers are sacred, representing love and honour, and are often used in ceremonies and dance. It is truly an honourable gift if you are blessed to receive one.

Deer is in the South. The Deer teaches us about generosity and sharing because it gives its meat for food and skin for drums, clothing, and regalia. Even today, when the Deer is hunted for food and clothing, we thank the Creator with an offering of tobacco.

Buffalo is in the West. The Buffalo teaches us to look within ourselves for guidance, and it guards the Western doorway to the spirit world. The Buffalo fed and clothed our ancestors. They followed the Buffalo and only hunted what they needed.

White Bear is in the North. The White Bear teaches us about fasting because of its long winter hibernation. When receiving a spirit name, the Conductor fasts until receiving a vision where the spirit name is revealed.

sweet grass

tobacco

sage

cedar

THE FOUR SACRED PLANTS

# THE SACRED PLANTS TEACH US ABOUT OUR CULTURE, HEALTH, AND SPIRITUALITY.

Tobacco is in the East. Tobacco was a natural plant, with no ingredients such as nicotine or tar to make it dangerous or addictive. It was used for offerings or giving thanks for the day's work, food, or guidance. It is burned in ceremonies as a prayer vessel to the Creator.

Cedar is in the South. The Cedar tree is a healing plant. Cedar is used to make shelter, transporatation, and regalia for West Coast Indigenous People, and medicine for many Indigenous People. We use the plant to make sacred teas and jelly.

Sage is in the West. Sage is considered a cleansing plant. It is often used in smudging, which means it is burned to invite positive energy, so we can see, hear, speak, and think in a good manner.

Sweet Grass is in the North. Sweet Grass is like the hair of Mother Earth. It is braided to remind us that as people we are strong when mind, body, and spirit are bound together as one in a balanced way.

THE FOUR NATIONS

white nation

black nation

yellow nation

red nation

# EACH NATION IS GIFTED
# IN A SPECIAL WAY.

The Four Nations teach us how to live in balance and harmony with others.
Each Nation contributes knowledge and appreciates the differences and gifts
of others, and this strengthens us all as people living on Earth.

The Yellow Nation, kind and innocent, is gifted with knowledge.
The Yellow Nation represents the knowledge to take a small object and
make it into something powerful.

The Red Nation, hard-working and helpful, is gifted with foresight.
The Red Nation represents the ability to foresee the future and see what
is needed to take care of others.

The Black Nation, free and peaceful, is gifted with insight.
The Black Nation is the keeper of the Western doorway through which
all people must go when they leave the Earth for the spirit world.

The White Nation, strong and wise, is gifted with swiftness and speed,
like that of the White Bear. The White Nation represents how listening to
an Elder's voice of wisdom will help the younger people who need guidance.

elder

adult

child

youth

THE FOUR STAGES OF LIFE

# EACH STAGE OF LIFE HAS A GIFT TO CONTRIBUTE TO THE COMMUNITY.

Child is in the East. This stage includes birth, infancy, and childhood, and represents innocence and curiosity. We are born innocent and as we grow, we learn to eat, speak, and walk. We learn what to do and what we like and dislike. We are curious about things we see in the world around us.

Youth is in the South. This stage includes childhood and adolescence, and represents seeking and questioning. As youths, we are always asking questions or even challenging adults. This can be a tough stage, as we want to be adults but are not yet able to do adult activities.

Adult is in the West. Adulthood represents care-taking and working hard to provide for family. Adults begin to understand that death and loss are important parts of life. Although being an adult may be hard, we do have our privileges and are learning forgiveness and peace.

Elder is in the North. This stage includes old age, and represents wisdom gained through experience. Elders and grandparents should always be given respect, as we have gained knowledge through living longer and learning more. We are wise from knowing and remembering all we have learned.

THE FOUR SACRED ASPECTS OF A HUMAN BEING

mind

body

spirit

heart

LEARNING · WONDERING · CURIOSITY · STORY · EXPERIENCE · THOUGHT · IMAGINATION · JUDGEMENT · FEELING · INSTINCT · REFLECTION · MEMORY

# THE SACRED ASPECTS OF HUMAN BEINGS HELP US UNDERSTAND OURSELVES.

Spirit is in the East. The Spirit enables us to see beyond the world and have vision so that knowledge is revealed. The young sons of our ancestors would fast in the woods and pray to see a vision. When the vision appeared, they then came out of the woods as young men.

Heart is in the South. The Heart allows us to feel and know through relationships with others and ourselves, including loving and accepting one another as we are. The Heart also reminds us to be kind as we nurture all living things on Mother Earth.

Body is in the West. The Body enables us to act, do, and know through physical responses. This reminds us that change happens in our bodies, just like it happens on Mother Earth. The Body reminds us to accept the cycle of birth and death as part of the fabric of life.

Mind is in the North. The Mind allows us to think, learn, and know through reflecting. Elders teach the young how to hunt, clothe and feed their families, and respect Mother Earth. An understanding of our culture and the world around us develops in our Minds.

sharing circle

the universe

life cycle

mother earth
THE SACRED CIRCLE

# THE SACRED CIRCLE REPRESENTS ALL OF THE MEDICINE WHEEL.

The Ojibwe People use the Medicine Wheel to see the Circle of Life, as it teaches and reflects circles in their many natural forms.

The planets dance around the sun in a circle, and this pattern is often imitated throughout the universe.

The tree, whose roots reach down to connect with Mother Earth, shows its age in circular form within its trunk.

Life cycles of birth and rebirth happen even in the tiny places all around us.

The drum, which is like the heartbeat of Mother Earth and all life, is shaped in a circle and played in a circle to keep the beat sacred.

# WE ARE ONE

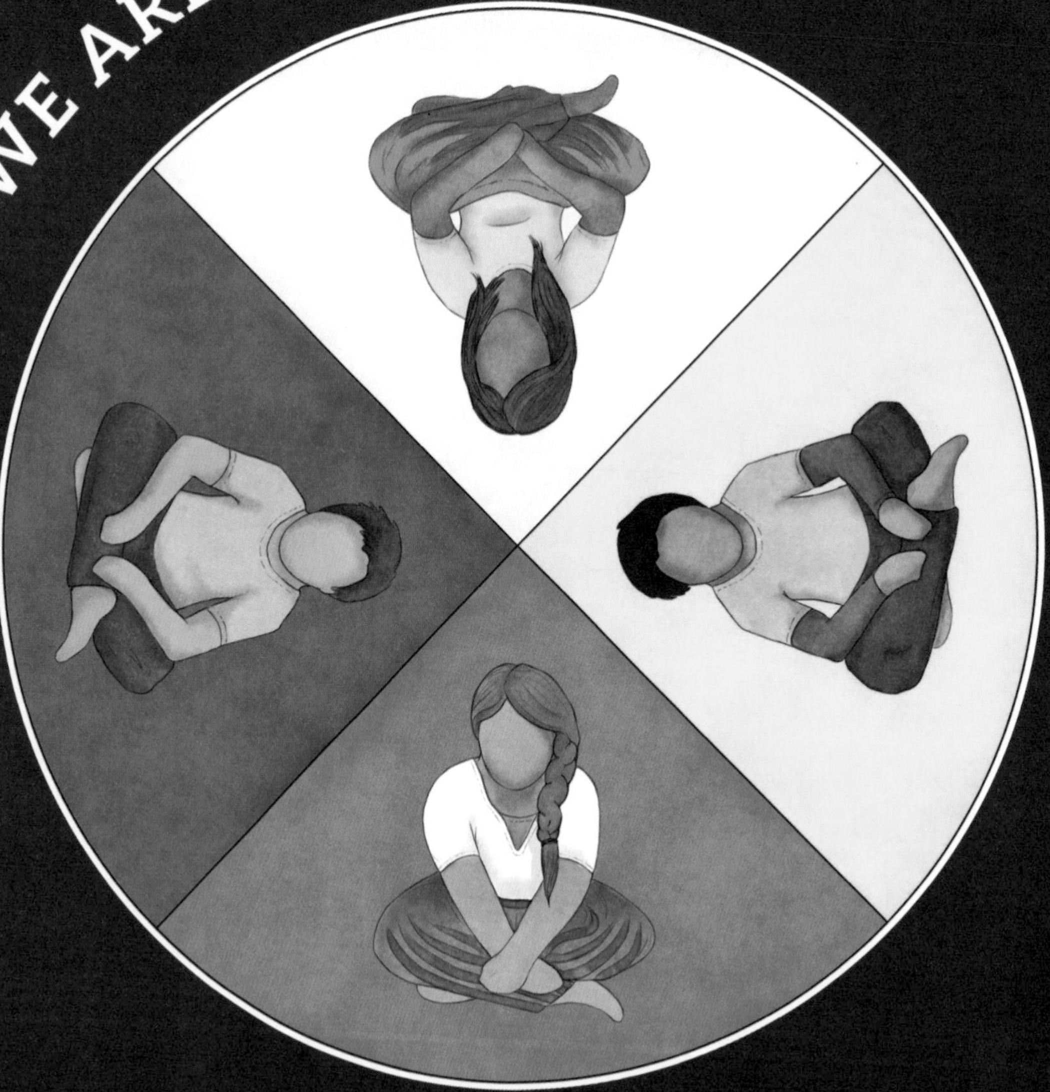

# WE ARE ONE.

The Medicine Wheel, in its various aspects, points out to us that we are all one,
all unified, and each an important part of this world. As we understand this, we realize that
we must work to maintain balance to keep other areas of the Wheel from suffering.

We appreciate the wisdom our ancestors had by using the Medicine Wheel
as a way of knowing about the world.

We recognize the insight it gives us as members of nature, communities, and families.

We acknowledge that we can show respect when facing each other in a circle,
whether in a meeting, at school, or just simply sharing the day.

# OJIBWE AND ENGLISH

## The Four Directions
Waabanong - East
Zhaawanong - South
Ningaabianong - West
Giiwedanong - North

## Stages of Life
Abinoojiins - Baby/Child
Kwezenhs/Niniis - Young Girl/Boy
Ikwe/Inini - Woman/Man
Gichi-Anishinabe - Elder

## The Four Sacred Colours
Zaawaa - Yellow
Miskwa - Red
Makade - Black
Waabishka - White

## The Four Sacred Animals
Migzi - Eagle
Wawashekshe - Deer
Mashkode-Biziki - Buffalo
Makwa - Bear

## The Four Elements
Nibi - Water
Ishkode - Fire
Aki - Earth
Noodin - Air/Wind

## The Four Aspects of Human Beings
Ode - Heart
Niiyaw - Body
Naagadawendamowin - Mind
Manidoo - Spirit

## The Four Sacred Plants

Gizhikaandagoons - Cedar

Bashkodejiibik - Sage

Bashkodemashkosiw - Sweet Grass

Asemaa - Tobacco

## The Four Seasons

Biboon - Winter

Ziigwan - Spring

Niibin - Summer

Dagwaagin - Autumn

## The Four Times of Day

Gigizheb - Morning

Naawakwe - Noon

Onaagoshig - Evening

Dibikad - Night

# VOWEL CHART

The seven vowels are a, aa, e, i, ii, o, oo.
Four of the vowels are long: aa, e, ii, oo.
Three of the vowels are short: a, i, o.
The long and short refer to the amount
of time you hold on to the sound
when you say it.

a    makes the "uh" sound as in
      the English word "**a**bout"

aa   makes the "ah" sound as in
      the English word "c**o**b"

e    makes the "ay" sound as in
      the English word "caf**é**"

i    makes the "ih" sound as in
      the English word "p**i**n"

ii   makes the "ee" sound as in
      the English word "s**ee**"

o    makes the "oh" sound as in
      the English word "**o**bey"

oo   makes the "oa" sound as in the
      English word "b**o**at," or the "oo"
      as in the English word "b**oo**t"

zh   makes the sound of the "s" in
      the English word "mea**s**ure"

*Note: Ojibwe spelling and pronunciation vary
across cultures and regions.*

Peppermint Toast Publishing supports local
charities and non-profit organizations.
With the sale of every book, we gladly pass on
profits to effect change in the lives of children.

Peppermint Toast Publishing is proud to be
giving 10% of the proceeds from every sale of
*All Creation Represented* to pediatric palliative
care being provided in British Columbia.
We are honoured to support places of comfort
and compassion where children with life-threatening
illnesses can experience the simple joy of being
a child, and families can cherish moments together.